CHARGRILLER
COOKBOOK

CHARGRILLER
COOKBOOK

TYPHOON

First published in 2002
for Typhoon International
by Hamlyn,
a division of Octopus Publishing Group Limited
2–4 Heron Quays, London, E14 4JP

ISBN 0 600 60637 6

Printed in China

ACKNOWLEDGEMENTS

Octopus Publishing Group Limited/Sandra Lane 11/Sean Myers front cover
bottom centre, 3, 7, 35/Philip Webb front cover top, front cover bottom left,
front cover bottom right, back cover, 15, 19, 23, 27, 31, 39, 43, 47, 51, 55, 59,
63

NOTES

1 Eggs should be large unless otherwise stated. This book contains some dishes
made with raw or lightly cooked eggs. It is prudent for more vulnerable people,
such as pregnant and nursing mothers, invalids, the elderly, babies and young
children, to avoid uncooked or lightly cooked dishes made with eggs.

2 Both metric and imperial measures have been given in all recipes. Use one set of
measurements only and not a mix of both.

3 Meat and poultry should be cooked thoroughly. To test if poultry is cooked,
pierce the flesh through the thickest part with a skewer or fork—the juices should
run clear, never pink or red. Keep refrigerated until ready for cooking.

4 This book contains dishes made with nuts and nut derivatives. It is advisable for
those with known allergic reactions to nuts and nut derivatives and those who
may be potentially vulnerable to these allergies, such as pregnant and nursing
mothers, invalids, the elderly, babies and children, to avoid dishes made with nuts
and nut oils. It is also prudent to check the labels of preprepared ingredients for
the possible inclusion of nut derivatives.

Contents

CHARGRILLER COOKBOOK

Chargrilling is a popular recent trend in cooking. It is an incredibly versatile method of cooking, and very easy. A chargriller looks like a frying pan with a ridged base and is used on top of the stove. Once you have bought a pan and had some practice, you will find chargrilling an effortless and enjoyable way of preparing food, and your pan will become an essential part of your kitchen equipment.

Successful chargrilling recreates the look and taste of food cooked over a barbecue, giving chargrilled foods a delicious smoky barbecued flavour. Chargrilling can be used for virtually any type of food, but is particularly successful with seafood, red and white meat, vegetables, fruit and some cheeses. The variety of dishes that can be cooked in a chargriller certainly adds to its appeal.

Chargrillers have been designed for cooking without the need to add oil or fat. This makes chargrilling a fat-free and moisture-retaining way of cooking – a popular notion with health-conscious cooks. And not only is it a healthy method, it is a fast one, too – something of particular relevance to busy cooks today.

The chargrilling process

The chargriller should always be heated through before you start to cook. This is done over a moderate to high heat so that the pan can heat up evenly; it takes 2–3 minutes. To test whether the chargriller is sufficiently hot, splash a few drops of water on the surface – they should sizzle violently and evaporate immediately; if they do not, continue heating the pan for a little longer. Alternatively, hold your hand approximately 2.5 cm (1 inch) above the surface of the chargriller, taking care not to burn it. If it feels hot, then the chargriller is ready for cooking.

When it is sufficiently hot, a chargriller acts like a branding iron when you first put food on it, and gives the food its characteristic chargrilled stripes, which

enhance its flavour. Thereafter, the food cooks at a steady, consistent heat, although it is sometimes necessary to turn down the heat a little to achieve this. Besides giving food the appetizing, chargrilled effect, the ridges on the bottom of the pan also lift the food slightly, so that it does not sit in its own juices.

Food will stick to the chargriller when it is first put on it, but once it has seared and a crust has formed, it can be moved or turned over. If the food still sticks when you come to turn it over, it is often best to leave it a little longer. This is particularly true of fish, fish cakes or burgers, and polenta; if you try to turn these too quickly they will stick to the pan or fall apart. The secret is not to have the heat under the chargriller so high that the food burns on the outside but remains raw on the inside. If you are cooking quite fatty foods, you may need to pour off the fatty juices occasionally.

Tips for successful chargrilling

Once you start chargrilling, everything happens quickly so make sure you have all your ingredients to hand.

Since chargrilling recipes tend to involve relatively few ingredients, the quality of these ingredients is crucial and influences the final flavour of the dish. The emphasis therefore is on crisp vegetables and fruit, and fresh meat and seafood. Remember to keep things simple. If you use too many ingredients, nothing will stand out and the simple perfection of chargrilling will be lost.

Thin and relatively tender foods are best suited to chargrilling – items that are no more than 5 cm (2 inches) thick work best as the centre will cook before the outside becomes dry and overcooked. Thicker cuts of chicken or pork, for example, can be seared on the chargriller and then moved to a preheated oven to cook all the way through.

Once cooked, serve chargrilled food with just a squeeze of lemon or lime juice or a drizzle of oil over the top. The choice of accompaniments, marinades and sauces can make chargrilling as simple or as spectacular as you like.

Marinades

Certain cuts of meat and fish benefit greatly from being marinated for a while before cooking. Marinades can be as simple as olive oil with a splash of lemon juice, perhaps with a little added yogurt, or they can be more heavily flavoured with garlic, chillies and other spices or honey.

Why use a marinade?

There are many reasons for marinating food, including the following:
• To allow the flavours to soak into the food
• To aromatize the food
• To tenderize lean meat and game
• To moisten meat or fish with juice or oil
• To enhance the flavour of meat, fish and vegetables
• To baste food

How long should I marinade for?

Although recipes often stipulate a length of time for marinating, food can be marinated for longer or shorter periods, as convenient. It makes no difference whether a marinade, for example a flavoured oil that is being used to moisten food or as a seasoning is added to food just before cooking or hours in advance. However, the longer that a food is soaked in a marinade intended to change its flavour or texture, the greater the effect will be – allow 4–24 hours. Foods marinating for 1–2 hours, or for a shorter time, can be left, covered, at room temperature, otherwise marinating should take place in the refrigerator. It is best to allow chilled food to return to room temperature before chargrilling (this takes about

30 minutes). Pour off the marinade and blot the food with kitchen paper to remove excess. Remove any larger items such as chopped onions or garlic from the surface of the meat or fish as they will burn on the chargriller. Towards the end of the cooking time, brush or sprinkle these marinade items on the food, if you like. Burned-on food residue can ruin the taste of the best ingredients, so be sure to clean the pan thoroughly after each use, following the instructions specific to your pan.

Wet Marinades

A wet marinade is usually made with oil, flavourings and an acidic liquid such as lemon juice, vinegar, wine, yogurt or pulped tomatoes. Marinate food in a non-reactive dish – one made of glass or ceramic – which holds the food snugly in a single layer. Sealable heavy-duty plastic bags are also an option for marinating. Any leftover marinade can be refrigerated in a covered jar for several weeks.

It is best not to put salt in marinades for meat as it draws out the juices and dries the meat. Instead, season chargrilled meat just before or after cooking.

To make the marinade combine all the ingredients in a bowl then add the meat, poultry or fish for marinating.

RED WINE MARINADE

150 ml (¼ pint) red wine
2 tablespoons lemon juice
1 onion, thinly sliced
1 carrot, thinly sliced
1 celery stick, finely chopped
1 parsley sprig
1 thyme sprig
1 bay leaf
6 black peppercorns, bruised
1 garlic clove, crushed

CITRUS MARINADE

finely grated rind and juice of 1 orange or
1 lemon, or 2 limes
1 tablespoon dark soy sauce
3 teaspoons clear honey
1 cm (½ inch) piece of fresh root ginger, peeled and
finely chopped
pepper

Dry Marinades

A dry marinade is a paste made from a blend of spices and dried or fresh herbs, which can be massaged into meat, poultry or fish. The idea is that the food should be permeated with your chosen blend of flavours, which will become stronger the longer it is left. The herbs and spices explode with flavour as they cook and form a delicious crusty exterior to the food.

Before applying a dry marinade, rinse or wipe clean the food to be marinated and blot dry with kitchen paper. Lightly oil all surfaces, then massage the spice rub into the food. Depending on the type of spice mixture, use 1–2 tablespoons per 500 g (1 lb) meat, poultry or fish. Let the food stand, covered, for 1 hour at room temperature before cooking to let the spices permeate the flesh.

There are many commercial spice combinations available but try making your own. A dry marinade made with fresh herbs and spices will keep in the refrigerator, if tightly covered, for up to three days. One made with dried seasonings can be stored in an airtight container for several weeks.

Making herb butters

Herb butters make scrumptious toppings for your char-grilled fish, meat and vegetable dishes, and they are really easy to make. Use the basic recipe that follows, or vary it according to what herbs you have available. Several examples are provided to give you some general guidelines. However it is great fun to experiment and create your own recipes. The butter should be cool and firm, but not taken straight from the refrigerator.

PARSLEY BUTTER

75 g/3 oz butter
I garlic clove, peeled
3 tablespoons chopped parsley
I tablespoon lemon juice
salt and pepper

1 Blend the butter in a food processor or blender to soften, then add the remaining ingredients.
2 Chill until firm. Alternatively, pound the butter in a mortar until it is creamy, then add the other ingredients gradually until they are well mixed. Chill until firm.

Variations

MINT BUTTER: use the same method with 2 tablespoons chopped mint.

TARRAGON BUTTER: use the same method with 2 tablespoons chopped tarragon.

MIXED HERB BUTTER: omit the garlic and use the same method with roughly ½ tablespoon chopped tarragon; ½ tablespoon chopped chervil; ½ tablespoon chopped dill; ½ tablespoon chopped chives and ½ tablespoon chopped mint, varying the balance to suit your taste.

Making flavoured oils

Olive oil is commonly used throughout this book but why not vary this by making your own flavoured oil. It is much more economical than buying the expensive versions sold in supermarkets. The method for making flavoured oil is very simple. The basic recipes given below use olive oil, but you can vary the oil according to your personal taste.

BASIL OIL

4 tablespoons chopped basil
450 ml/¾ pint olive oil

1 Pound the basil briefly in a mortar. Add a little of the oil and pound again. Add the rest of the oil gradually and pour into a wide-mouthed glass bottle. Seal tightly.
2 Keep the oil for 2 weeks before using, shaking the bottle every 2 or 3 days.

AROMATIC OIL

450 ml/¾ pint olive oil
2 branches rosemary
6 thyme sprigs
I large garlic clove, peeled and halved
I green chilli pepper
5–6 small red chilli peppers
6 black peppercorns
6 juniper berries

1 Pour the oil into a clear glass bottle with a tightly-fitting cork. Wash the herbs thoroughly and dry them with kitchen paper.
2 Drop the herbs into the oil with the remaining ingredients. Seal tightly.
3 Keep the oil for 2 weeks before using, shaking the bottle every 2 or 3 days.

POTATOES WITH FENNEL AND OLIVE OIL

This vegetable dish is particularly good served with salmon steaks,
since fennel and fish are a winning combination.

500 g (1 lb) pink new potatoes, halved
2 fennel heads, cut into thin wedges
a drizzle of olive oil
sea salt and pepper

1 Heat the chargriller. Chargrill the potatoes for 10 minutes on each side or until soft when tested with a knife. Remove and keep warm – allowing the potatoes to sit for 10 minutes to steam in their skins – while you continue to chargrill the rest of the potatoes. Chargrill the fennel for 3–4 minutes on each side. Add to the cooked potatoes, drizzle with olive oil and season well with salt and pepper.

Serves 4
Preparation time: 5–10 minutes
Cooking time: 30 minutes

HERB FRITTERS WITH YOGURT DIP

These fritters make great nibbling food. The mix can be made in advance
but try and cook the fritters just before serving to retain the flavours of the fresh chopped herbs.

150 g (5 oz) mozzarella cheese, finely chopped
1 bunch of basil, chopped
1 bunch of flat leaf parsley, chopped
1 bunch of chives, chopped
1 garlic clove, finely chopped
100 g (3½ oz) cooked mashed potato
1 egg, beaten
sea salt and pepper
chives, to garnish

YOGURT DIP:
200 g (7 oz) Greek yogurt
1 shallot, finely chopped
1 bunch of mint, finely chopped
1 garlic clove, finely chopped

1 Place the chopped mozzarella in a mixing bowl. Add the chopped herbs and mix well. Add the garlic, mashed potato and beaten egg. Season with salt and pepper and mix well.
2 Divide the mixture into 12 pieces, shape into balls and flatten slightly. Heat the chargriller.
3 Place the fritters on the chargriller and cook in batches for 4–5 minutes on each side. Keep the chargrilled fritters warm until they are all cooked.
4 To make the dip, place the yogurt, shallot, mint and garlic in a bowl. Mix well and serve with the fritters. Serve the fritters garnished with chives.

Serves 4
Preparation time: 15 minutes
Cooking time: 20 minutes

SPICY COURGETTE FRITTERS

500 g (1 lb) courgettes, grated
1 egg, beaten
2 tablespoons plain flour
1 chilli, deseeded and chopped
1 garlic clove, crushed
75 g (3 oz) Cheddar cheese, grated
125 g (4 oz) smoked salmon
125 ml (4 fl oz) cream cheese
sea salt and pepper
sprigs of dill, to garnish

1 Heat the chargriller. Squeeze the excess moisture out of the grated courgettes – the best way to do this is to place all the courgettes in a clean tea towel and squeeze well.
2 Mix together the egg and flour until smooth, add the chilli and garlic, mix well and season with salt and pepper.
3 Add the egg mixture to the grated courgette and gently mix to combine. Spoon the fritter mixture on to the chargriller and flatten it with a palette knife. Allow the fritters to cook for 4–5 minutes, then turn them over and cook for a further 4–5 minutes. Do not disturb them while they are cooking as a crust needs to form on the cooking side, otherwise they will be difficult to turn.
4 Keep the cooked fritters warm and repeat until all the mixture has been used. Serve the fritters between layers of smoked salmon and cream cheese, and garnished with dill sprigs.

Serves 4
Preparation time: 10 minutes
Cooking time: 20 minutes

BUTTERNUT PUMPKIN WITH PARMESAN

Not only is this dish sensational to look at, it is also delicious to eat.
Pumpkin is a great accompaniment to roasts, especially chicken, and children love it for its sweetness.
The butternut, known as the Queen of Pumpkins because it is the sweetest of all,
can be bought all year round and keeps well in a cool place.

**1 kg (2 lb) butternut pumpkin, deseeded
and cut into small wedges or slices
75 g (3 oz) butter
150 g (5 oz) Parmesan cheese
sea salt and pepper**

1 Heat the chargriller, add the pumpkin in batches and cook for about 10 minutes on each side. As the pumpkin wedges are cooked, transfer them to a large plate and keep warm.
2 Melt the butter in a small pan and heat it until it just begins to brown, to give a rich, nutty flavour. Pour the butter over the cooked pumpkin and season with salt and pepper. Using a vegetable peeler, shave the Parmesan directly on to the pumpkin and serve immediately, or when it has cooled a little, but before the butter hardens.

Serves 4
Preparation time: 10 minutes
Cooking time: 35 minutes

NAAN VEGETABLE SANDWICH

You can make all sorts of variations on this sandwich, adding cheese,
bacon, chargrilled fish or chicken, for example, and different dressings can also be used.

2 peppers, cored, deseeded and sliced
1 small aubergine, sliced into rounds
2 courgettes, sliced
4 flat mushrooms
1 oak leaf lettuce, washed
1 naan bread
2 garlic cloves
1 tablespoon olive oil
1 tablespoon water
3 tablespoons fromage frais
1 tablespoon chopped parsley
sea salt and pepper

1 Heat the chargriller. Place the peppers on the chargriller and cook for 5 minutes, turning occasionally. Arrange the aubergine slices on the pan and cook for 3 minutes on each side. Add to the peppers, then put the courgettes on the pan and cook for 5 minutes, turning occasionally. Finally, chargrill the mushrooms. Keep all the vegetables warm.

2 Cut the naan into 4 portions, slice each one in half and chargrill the soft sides for 2 minutes or until toasted. Rub the bread with garlic and spoon a little oil over each toasted side.

3 Mix together the water, fromage frais and parsley and season with salt and pepper.

4 Place the lettuce leaves and chargrilled vegetables on the bread and season with salt and pepper. Drizzle with the fromage frais dressing and top with the second piece of naan.

Serves 4
Preparation time: 10 minutes
Cooking time: 30 minutes

AUBERGINES WITH LEMON PESTO

This dish can be made in advance, on the day of eating, but should not be refrigerated.

4 aubergines, sliced into rounds, or baby
aubergines, sliced lengthways
1 large bunch of basil
75 g (3 oz) pine nuts, toasted
1 garlic clove
75 g (3 oz) Parmesan cheese, grated
grated rind of 2 lemons
4 tablespoons lemon juice
3 tablespoons olive oil
sea salt and pepper

1 Heat the chargriller. Place the aubergines on the pan and cook for 3 minutes on each side, then remove them and arrange on a warmed serving dish. Repeat until all the aubergines are cooked.
2 To make the pesto, place the basil, pine nuts, garlic, Parmesan, lemon rind and juice, olive oil and salt and pepper in a food processor or blender and process until smooth. Drizzle the lemon pesto over the aubergines and serve with crusty bread.

Serves 4
Preparation time: 10 minutes
Cooking time: 18 minutes

CHARGRILLED SWEET POTATO CHIPS

Sweet potatoes can be cooked in exactly the same way as ordinary potatoes – roasted, mashed, fried or boiled.

750 g (1½ lb) sweet potatoes, peeled
sea salt and pepper

DIP:
150 g (5 oz) strained Greek yogurt
1 shallot, finely diced
1 cool red chilli, deseeded and finely diced
1 bunch of coriander chopped
few drops of Tabasco sauce

1 Cut the sweet potato into slices 2.5 cm (1 inch) wide, then cut the slices into 2.5 cm (1 inch) chips. Heat the chargriller and put on a single layer of chips, leaving a little space between each one. Cook for about 3 minutes on each side, or 12 minutes in total. Remove from the chargriller and keep warm. Repeat until all the sweet potato is cooked. Sprinkle the chips with sea salt and pepper and arrange on a large platter, leaving room for a dipping bowl.
2 To make the dip, mix the yogurt, shallot, chilli, coriander and Tabasco in a small bowl with salt and pepper to taste. Arrange the dip on the same plate as the potato chips.

Serves 4
Preparation time: 15 minutes
Cooking time: about 30 minutes

PEAR AND STILTON SALAD

The combination of pear and Stilton, used here to good effect, must have been made in heaven!

4 pears
4 tablespoons lemon juice
250 g (8 oz) baby spinach or mixed salad leaves
4 chopped walnuts
250 g (8 oz) Stilton cheese, crumbled
4 tablespoons walnut oil

1 Heat the chargriller.

2 Cut each pear into quarters and remove the core, then slice each quarter in half. Place the slices of pear on the chargriller and cook on each side for 1 minute. Remove the pears and sprinkle them with the lemon juice.

3 Pile the spinach or mixed salad leaves on a large platter and arrange the pears on top. Sprinkle with the walnuts and crumbled Stilton and spoon the walnut oil over the salad. Serve immediately.

Serves 4
Preparation time: 10 minutes
Cooking time: 5 minutes

Warm Salad of Beetroot and Parsnips

Beetroot and parsnips go together surprisingly well, as well as making an attractive visual contrast.
This salad is ideal for serving with fish.

500 g (1 lb) raw beetroot, peeled and cut into 1 cm (½ inch) thick slices
500 g (1 lb) parsnips, peeled and cut into 1 cm (½ inch) thick slices
4 tablespoons soured cream
3 tablespoons water
1 bunch of dill, chopped
sea salt and pepper

1 Heat the chargriller. Chargrill the beetroot slices on each side for 4–5 minutes, then remove and keep warm. Repeat until all the slices are cooked.

2 Chargrill the slices of parsnip on each side for 4–5 minutes, remove and add to the beetroot. Repeat until all the slices are cooked.

3 Mix together the soured cream, water and dill and season with salt and pepper. Drizzle over the chargrilled beetroot and parsnips.

Serves 4
Preparation time: 10 minutes
Cooking time: 20 minutes

CHARGRILLED LAMB IN NAAN BREAD WITH MINT SALAD

750 g (1½ lb) minced lamb
1 bunch of parsley, chopped
1 onion, chopped
1 garlic clove, crushed
dash of Tabasco sauce
1 egg, beaten
4 small naan breads
1 red onion, sliced
3 tomatoes, halved and finely sliced
1 large bunch of mint, chopped
2 tablespoons olive oil
2 tablespoons lemon juice
sea salt and pepper

1 Mix together the lamb, parsley, onion, garlic, Tabasco, egg and salt and pepper. Shape into 8 sausages that will fit into the naan breads.

2 Heat the chargriller. Place the lamb sausages on the chargriller and cook for 6–9 minutes. Take care when turning the sausages – it is important to get a good crust on the outside, so that they don't break when they are turned over.

3 Combine the onion, tomatoes, mint, olive oil and lemon juice and season to taste with salt and pepper. Open the naan breads carefully and make a pocket for the filling.

4 Place the naan breads under a moderately hot conventional grill and cook on each side until lightly browned. Divide the salad among the naans and add the lamb sausages. Serve immediately.

Serves 4
Preparation time: 20 minutes
Cooking time: 12 minutes

LIVER AND BACON WITH ROASTED TOMATO CHUTNEY

3 tablespoons olive oil
750 g (1½ lb) tomatoes, halved and green cores removed
1 red onion, sliced
1 garlic clove, crushed and chopped
50 g (2 oz) raisins
50 g (2 oz) brown sugar
2–3 tablespoons white wine vinegar
1 teaspoon chopped rosemary
1 teaspoon black mustard seeds
8 rashers of smoked streaky bacon, rinded
4 slices calves' liver, about 125 g (4 oz) each
sea salt and pepper
rosemary sprigs, to garnish

1 Spoon 2 tablespoons of the olive oil into a roasting tin and heat in a preheated oven, 220°C (425°F), Gas Mark 7. Add the tomatoes, turn them in the oil to coat well, and place the tin at the top of the oven. Roast for 40 minutes, or until the tomatoes begin to darken around the edges.

2 Heat the remaining olive oil in a frying pan and add the onion and garlic. Fry over a low heat for 5 minutes, then add the raisins, brown sugar, vinegar, rosemary, mustard seeds and season with salt and pepper. Mix well and simmer for 2 minutes. Stir in the roasted tomatoes, then remove the pan from the heat.

3 Heat the chargriller, add the bacon rashers and cook until crispy, about 2 minutes on each side. Keep warm. Place the calves' liver on the chargriller and cook for 2 minutes on each side for pink, or 4 minutes for well done. Garnish the liver and bacon with rosemary sprigs and serve immediately with the tomato chutney.

Serves 4
Preparation time: 10 minutes
Cooking time: about 1 hour

SAUSAGES WITH MUSTARD MASH

8 speciality sausages
2 onions, cut into wedges, roots left intact

MUSTARD MASH:
I kg (2 lb) potatoes, quartered but left unpeeled
75 g (3 oz) butter
I tablespoon wholegrain mustard
3 teaspoons English mustard
I garlic clove, crushed
I large bunch of parsley, chopped
dash of olive oil
sea salt and pepper

I Heat the chargriller.

2 Put the potatoes into a saucepan of cold water, bring to the boil and simmer for 15 minutes.

3 While the potatoes are cooking, put the sausages on the chargriller and cook for 10 minutes, turning to get an even colour. Add the onion wedges and cook for 6–7 minutes with the sausages.

4 When the potatoes are cooked, drain them well and return to the pan. Place the pan over a low heat to allow any excess water to steam away, without colouring the potatoes. Remove the pan from the heat. Peel the potatoes, then mash them well; add the butter, the wholegrain and English mustards, garlic and salt and pepper, and continue to mash. Taste the potato and add more mustard if liked. Finally, add the parsley and a dash of olive oil and stir well.

5 Serve the sausage and mash with the chargrilled onion wedges.

Serves 4
Preparation time: 10 minutes
Cooking time: 25 minutes

CHARGRILLED GAMMON WITH APRICOT SALSA

This is a simple yet effective recipe, and the apricot salsa is the perfect accompaniment for the gammon. If fresh apricots are not available, chop up some ready-to-eat dried apricots.

4 x 175 g (6 oz) gammon steaks

APRICOT SALSA:
250 g (8 oz) fresh apricots, stoned and chopped
grated rind and juice of 1 lime
2 teaspoons fresh root ginger, finely diced
2 teaspoons clear honey
1 tablespoon olive oil
2 tablespoons chopped sage
spring onions, chopped
sea salt and pepper

1 Heat the chargriller. Add the gammon steaks in batches and cook for 4 minutes on each side. Keep warm until all the steaks are cooked.

2 While the gammon steaks are cooking, make the salsa. In a small bowl, mix together the apricots, lime rind and juice, ginger, honey, olive oil and sage. Crush the mixture with the back of a fork. Add the spring onions, season with salt and pepper and mix well.

3 Serve the gammon steaks immediately, topped with the apricot salsa.

Serves 4
Preparation time: 15 minutes
Cooking time: 16 minutes

PORK ESCALOPES CHARGRILLED WITH PEACH CHUTNEY

This peach chutney is a lovely accompaniment to meat. Use fresh peaches when they are in season, otherwise use dried ones, and soak them for a couple of hours. If you like your food hot and spicy, add a sprinkling of dried chillies to the chutney.

4 x 175 g (6 oz) pork escalopes, halved

PEACH CHUTNEY:
4 fresh peaches
1 tablespoon olive oil
1 onion, sliced
1 tablespoon vinegar
2 tablespoons brown sugar
2 teaspoons mustard seeds
sea salt and pepper
oregano sprigs, to garnish

1 First make the peach chutney. Bring a saucepan of water to the boil and make a cross in the skin of the peaches. Plunge the peaches into the boiling water for 10 seconds. Lift them out with a slotted spoon and peel away the skin. Cut the peach flesh away from the stone and into wedges.

2 Gently heat the oil in a saucepan, add the sliced onion and cook until soft. Add the peaches with the vinegar, sugar and mustard seeds and season to taste with salt and pepper. Let the mixture simmer gently for 10 minutes, watching carefully that it does not stick on the bottom of the pan. Add a little water if it looks like drying out.

3 Heat the chargriller. Cook the escalopes for 4–5 minutes on each side depending on their thickness, or until they are cooked.

4 Serve the escalopes with the peach chutney and garnished with oregano sprigs. Roasted root vegetables, such as beetroot, parsnips, turnips, carrots and potatoes, make a good accompaniment.

Serves 4
Preparation time: 10 minutes
Cooking time: 20 minutes

DUCK WITH ORANGES AND CRANBERRIES

4 Barbary duck breasts
2 oranges
125 g (4 oz) cranberries
50 g (2 oz) light brown sugar
1 tablespoon clear honey
sea salt and pepper

1 Heat the chargriller. Score the skin of the duck breasts through to the flesh – this allows the fat to be released and the skin to go crispy.

2 Place the duck breasts on the chargriller and cook them on the skin side for 6–10 minutes and then on the other side for 4–6 minutes.

3 Meanwhile, remove the rind and pith from the oranges, then segment them.

4 Place the oranges, cranberries and sugar in a saucepan, season with a little salt and pepper and simmer to soften the cranberries. Finally, add the honey to the sauce.

5 Remove the duck breasts from the chargriller, cut them into slices and serve with the orange and cranberry sauce.

Serves 4
Preparation time: 10 minutes
Cooking time: 20 minutes

TURKEY WITH CITRUS CHILLI SAUCE

grated rind and juice of 2 lemons
125 g (4 oz) sugar
1 onion, finely chopped
2 chillies, finely chopped
1 garlic clove, crushed
100 ml (3½ fl oz) water
4 x 175 g (6 oz) turkey escalopes
sea salt and pepper
basmati rice, to serve
torn basil leaves, to garnish

1 Place the lemon rind and juice, sugar, onion, chillies, garlic and water in a small saucepan and simmer gently for 15 minutes. Watch this mixture carefully while it cooks, as it will burn easily.
2 Heat the chargriller. Season the turkey escalopes well with salt and pepper, place on the chargriller and cook for 5 minutes on each side.
3 To serve, arrange a bed of rice on 4 warmed plates and add the escalopes. Pour over the chilli sauce and garnish with the basil leaves.

Serves 4
Preparation time: 15 minutes
Cooking time: 25 minutes

CHARGRILLED TANDOORI CHICKEN

4 boneless, skinless chicken breasts
4 tablespoons tandoori paste
2 onions, sliced
1 bunch of coriander, chopped

TO GARNISH:
lemon wedges
coriander sprigs

1 Make 3 slashes in each chicken breast.

2 Rub the chicken with the tandoori paste and leave to marinate, preferably overnight.

3 Heat the chargriller. Place the chicken breasts on the chargriller and cook for 8–10 minutes on each side, allowing a little charred colour to develop. Add the sliced onions and chargrill until slightly coloured.

4 When the chicken and onions are cooked, stir the chopped coriander into the onions. Serve the chicken with the onion and coriander mixture and garnish with lemon wedges and coriander sprigs.

Serves 4
Preparation time: 10 minutes, plus marinating
Cooking time: 20 minutes

LEMON CHICKEN WITH SPAGHETTI

4 lemons
4 x 125 g (4 oz) skinless chicken
breast fillets
I bunch of oregano, chopped
300 g (10 oz) spaghetti
I bunch of parsley, chopped
2 tablespoons olive oil
sea salt and pepper

I Thinly slice 3 of the lemons, setting aside 8 large slices. Grate the rind and squeeze the juice from the fourth lemon, and set aside.

2 Using a sharp knife, make a long slit in the middle of each chicken fillet. Fill each chicken pocket with some of the smaller lemon slices, some chopped oregano leaves and salt and pepper.

3 Heat the chargriller. Sandwich each chicken fillet between 2 of the large reserved lemon slices with an oregano sprig. Place the chicken on the chargriller and cook for 8 minutes on each side – try to keep the lemon with the chicken so that the chicken is suffused with lemon.

4 Meanwhile, bring a large saucepan of lightly salted water to the boil. Cook the spaghetti for 12 minutes, or according to the packet instructions. Drain well, then toss with the grated lemon rind and juice, the chopped parsley, olive oil and salt and pepper. Serve with the lemon chicken.

Serves 4
Preparation time: 15 minutes
Cooking time: about 20 minutes

MONKFISH WITH LEEKS AND PARMESAN

I leek, finely sliced
125 g (4 oz) Parmesan cheese,
finely grated
750 g (1½ lb) prepared monkfish fillets, cut
into slices 1.5 cm (¾ inch) thick
I egg white, lightly beaten
sea salt and pepper
lemon wedges, to serve

1 Heat the chargriller.

2 Mix together the leek and Parmesan and season to taste with salt and pepper.

3 Pat the slices of monkfish dry with kitchen paper. Dip the monkfish slices into the egg white, then roll them in the leek and Parmesan mixture. Put the monkfish on the chargriller and cook for 3–4 minutes on each side. Serve with the lemon wedges.

Serves 4
Preparation time: 10 minutes
Cooking time: 10 minutes

CHARGRILLED SALMON WITH A CHILLI CRUST

The chilli crust not only looks good but also imparts some delicious flavours to the fish.

3 teaspoons crushed dried chillies
8 teaspoons sesame seeds
1 large bunch of parsley, finely chopped
4 x 150 g (5 oz) salmon fillets, skinned
1 egg white, lightly beaten
sea salt and pepper

TO SERVE:
1 lime, cut into wedges and chargrilled
noodles (optional)

1 Heat the chargriller.

2 Mix together the crushed dried chillies, sesame seeds, parsley and salt and pepper, and spread out on a plate. Put the beaten egg white on another plate.

3 Dip the salmon fillets into the egg white, then coat them in the crust mixture. Pat the mix on to the salmon to ensure an even covering.

4 Place the salmon fillets on the hot chargriller and cook for 4 minutes on each side, turning them carefully with a palette knife and keeping the crust on the fish. Serve the salmon with the chargrilled lime quarters and noodles, if liked.

Serves 4
Preparation time: 10 minutes
Cooking time: 10 minutes

SNAPPER WITH CARROTS AND CARAWAY SEEDS

500 g (1 lb) carrots, sliced
2 teaspoons caraway seeds
4 x 175 g (6 oz) snapper fillets
2 oranges
1 bunch of coriander, leaves roughly chopped, plus extra to garnish
4 tablespoons olive oil
sea salt and pepper

1 Heat the chargriller and cook the carrots for 3 minutes on each side, adding the caraway seeds for the last 2 minutes of cooking. Remove from the chargriller and keep warm.
2 Cook the snapper fillets on the chargriller for 3 minutes on each side.
3 Squeeze the juice from one of the oranges and cut the other into quarters. Place the orange quarters on the chargriller and cook until browned.
4 Add the coriander to the carrots and mix well. Season to taste with salt and pepper and stir in the olive oil and orange juice. Serve the carrots with the cooked fish and chargrilled orange wedges. Garnish with the extra chopped coriander.

Serves 4
Preparation time: 10 minutes
Cooking time: 15 minutes

CHARGRILLED SEA BASS WITH SPICY SALSA

This spicy tomato salsa provides a good contrast in both flavour and texture
to the smooth meaty flesh of chargrilled sea bass.

4 x 175 g (6 oz) sea bass fillets

SPICY SALSA:
4 plum tomatoes, skinned and deseeded
I chilli, finely chopped
2 garlic cloves, finely chopped
**50 g (2 oz) black olives, pitted and
finely chopped**
I shallot, finely chopped
4 tablespoons olive oil
4 tablespoons lemon juice
sea salt and pepper
parsley sprigs, to garnish

TO SERVE:
freshly cooked tagliatelle
spinach salad
lemon wedges

I To make the spicy salsa, roughly chop the tomatoes and place them in a large bowl. Add the finely chopped chilli, garlic, olives and shallot, the olive oil, lemon juice and a little salt and pepper. Mix well, cover and set aside for at least 1 hour to let the flavours blend.

2 Heat the chargriller. Cook the sea bass fillets for 3–4 minutes on each side, then garnish with the parsley. Serve with the spicy salsa, tagliatelle, a spinach salad and lemon wedges for squeezing.

Serves 4
Preparation time: 15 minutes, plus marinating
Cooking time: 6–8 minutes

SESAME TUNA WITH DIPPING SAUCE

575 g (1 lb 3 oz) tuna fillet or 2 fillets
weighing about 300 g (10 oz)
each, skinned
3 tablespoons black sesame seeds
3 tablespoons white sesame seeds, toasted
1 egg white
sea salt
cooked spinach, to serve

DIPPING SAUCE:
100 ml (3½ fl oz) soy sauce
1 chilli, finely chopped
1 garlic clove, crushed

1 Pat the tuna fillet dry with kitchen paper. Mix together the black and white sesame seeds and pour on to a plate. Tip the egg white into a dish and whisk lightly.

2 Dip the tuna fillets into the egg white to coat it all over, then dip them into the sesame seeds. Pat the sesame seeds on to the tuna to coat the fish thoroughly with the seeds.

3 Heat the chargriller. Slice the tuna diagonally and place the slices on the hot chargriller and cook for 3 minutes on each side for rare, 5 minutes for medium or 8 minutes for well done.

4 To make the dipping sauce, combine the soy sauce, finely chopped chilli and the crushed garlic and pour into 4 little dishes. Season the tuna slices with salt, then arrange on individual plates with cooked spinach. Serve the sauce separately.

Serves 4
Preparation time: 10 minutes
Cooking time: 6–16 minutes

MARINATED GINGER AND GARLIC GREEN PRAWNS

24 raw tiger prawns, peeled, heads removed and deveined
5 cm (2 inch) piece of fresh root ginger, peeled and finely diced
4 large garlic cloves, crushed
1 green chilli, deseeded and finely chopped
1 bunch of spring onions, cut into 5 cm (2 inch) lengths
150 g (5 oz) rice noodles
1 tablespoon sesame oil
2 tablespoons soy sauce
1 bunch of coriander, chopped
grated rind and juice of 1 lime
sea salt and pepper

1 Place the prawns in a glass dish. Add the ginger, garlic and chilli. Mix well, cover and leave to marinate in the refrigerator for at least 2 hours. If time is short, marinate them for 1 hour but do not put them in the refrigerator.

2 Cut the spring onions into 5 cm (2 inch) lengths, then cut the lengths into thin strips. Place them in a bowl of iced water, where they will become curly – the longer they are left and the colder the water, the curlier they will become.

3 Heat the chargriller. Put the prawns on the chargriller and cook for 3 minutes on each side.

4 While the prawns are cooking, bring a saucepan of lightly salted water to the boil. Add the rice noodles and cook for 2 minutes then drain well. Return the noodles to the saucepan, add the sesame oil, soy sauce, coriander, lime rind and juice, and salt and pepper to taste, and toss well.

5 Drain the spring onions, add to the prawns and cook for 30 seconds. Arrange the noodles on individual plates, add the prawns and spring onions and serve immediately.

Serves 4
Preparation time: 20 minutes, plus marinating
Cooking time: 10 minutes

CHARGRILLED TIGER PRAWNS WITH MINT AND LEMON

750 g (1½ lb) raw tiger prawns, heads
removed, peeled and deveined
1 large bunch of mint, chopped
2 garlic cloves, crushed
8 tablespoons lemon juice
sea salt and pepper
mint leaves, to garnish

1 Place the prawns in a glass mixing bowl.
2 Add the mint, garlic and lemon juice, season to taste with salt and pepper and leave to marinate for at least 30 minutes.
3 Heat the chargriller. Place the prawns on the chargriller with the marinade and cook for 2–3 minutes on each side. Serve the prawns garnished with the mint leaves.

Serves 4
Preparation time: 10 minutes, plus marinating
Cooking time: 4–6 minutes

SEARED SCALLOPS ON MIXED LEAVES WITH LIME DRESSING

Scallops go particularly well with the citrus tang of a lime dressing and warm crusty bread.

16 large scallops, cleaned
grated rind and juice of 2 limes
3 tablespoons olive oil
1 bunch of dill, chopped
sea salt and pepper
1 large bag of mixed leaves, to serve

1 Heat the chargriller. Dry the scallops well with kitchen paper to remove excess water.

2 Place the scallops on the chargriller and cook for 3 minutes on each side. Mix together the lime juice and rind, olive oil and chopped dill, and season with salt and pepper to taste.

3 Toss the salad in the lime dressing and arrange on 4 plates. Place the scallops on the salad and garnish with a little dressing.

Serves 4
Preparation time: 10–15 minutes
Cooking time: 6 minutes

CHARGRILLED COURGETTES AND PEPPERS WITH PENNE AND BRIE

4 courgettes, sliced
I red pepper, cored, deseeded and sliced
I green pepper, cored, deseeded and sliced
I yellow pepper, cored, deseeded and sliced
500 g (I lb) dried penne
175 g (6 oz) ripe Brie, diced
2 tablespoons olive oil
I bunch of dill, chopped
sea salt and pepper

I Heat the chargriller.

2 Place the courgettes and peppers on the chargriller and cook for 5 minutes, in batches, turning occasionally.

3 Meanwhile, cook the penne in a pan of lightly salted boiling water for 8 minutes. Drain well and return to the pan.

4 Add the chargrilled vegetables, diced Brie, olive oil and dill to the cooked pasta. Season to taste with salt and pepper, mix well and cook over a low heat for 5 minutes then serve immediately.

Serves 4
Preparation time: 5 minutes
Cooking time: 15 minutes

CHARGRILLED VEGETABLES WITH CREAMED POLENTA

Polenta is a cornmeal porridge traditionally eaten in northern Italy.
It is very versatile and can be used for many different dishes.

1 red pepper, cored, deseeded and quartered
4 baby aubergines, quartered
4 baby courgettes, quartered
8 baby sweetcorn
8 baby leeks
1 red onion, cut into wedges, root left intact
8 baby tomatoes
600 ml (1 pint) water
150 g (5 oz) instant polenta flour
50 g (2 oz) butter, plus a little extra for greasing
2 tablespoons olive oil, plus a little extra for drizzling
1 bunch of oregano, chopped
175 g (6 oz) soft rindless goats' cheese
sea salt and pepper

1 Heat the chargriller and chargrill all the vegetables for 2–4 minutes on each side. Keep warm in a large dish.

2 Heat the water to a gentle boil, pour in the polenta and beat well for 1–2 minutes until it becomes a smooth paste. Reduce the heat and cook the polenta for 6–8 minutes until it thickens, stirring constantly so that it does not stick on the bottom of the pan.

3 Add the butter, olive oil and oregano, and season to taste with salt and pepper. Mix well. The polenta should have the consistency of soft mashed potatoes.

4 Grease a large serving dish with butter, spread the polenta over the bottom and arrange the chargrilled vegetables over it. Crumble the goats' cheese over the top, drizzle with olive oil and place under a hot conventional grill until the cheese has melted. Serve with a leafy salad, if liked.

Serves 4
Preparation time: 15 minutes
Cooking time: 30 minutes

CHARGRILLED VEGETABLES WITH AÏOLI

selection of seasonal vegetables, such as asparagus, peppers, red onion, fennel, aubergines, potatoes, baby leeks and courgettes

AÏOLI:
2 egg yolks
½ teaspoon Dijon mustard
2 garlic cloves, crushed
2 tablespoons lemon juice
175 ml (6 fl oz) olive oil
sea salt and pepper

1 First make the aïoli. Place the egg yolks, Dijon mustard, garlic and lemon juice in a food processor or blender and, with the motor running, very slowly drizzle in the olive oil – a few drops to begin with and then in a thin stream. Process until the mixture is thick. Season to taste with salt and pepper. Turn into a serving bowl and set aside.

2 Cut the vegetables into chunks, wedges or slices. Heat the chargriller.

3 Chargrill the vegetables, turning them frequently, then keep them warm in a low oven. Most vegetables will take about 4–5 minutes, but you should allow longer for potato slices.

4 Serve the chargrilled vegetables with the aïoli.

Serves 4
Preparation time: 30 minutes
Cooking time: 20–30 minutes

CHARGRILLED VEGETABLE RISOTTO

1 red onion, sliced
125 g (4 oz) asparagus, chopped
2 courgettes, sliced
4 mushrooms, sliced
125 g (4 oz) butternut pumpkin, peeled and diced
1 litre (1¾ pints) vegetable or chicken stock
125 g (4 oz) butter
1 tablespoon olive oil
1 garlic clove, crushed
1 onion, finely chopped
300 g (10 oz) arborio rice
75 ml (3 fl oz) dry white wine
1 tablespoon chopped sage
125 g (4 oz) Parmesan cheese, cut into shavings
1 tablespoon chopped sage, to garnish

1 Heat the chargriller and chargrill the red onion, asparagus, courgettes, mushrooms and pumpkin, cooking them all for about 5 minutes, and turning them occasionally. You will have to do this in batches.

2 Meanwhile, cook the rice. Pour the stock into a saucepan and bring to a simmer.

3 Heat half the butter with the oil in a large heavy-based saucepan, add the garlic and chopped onion and cook for 3 minutes. Do not allow to brown.

4 Add the rice to the pan and stir well to coat the grains with the butter mixture, then pour in enough hot stock to cover the rice, keeping the pan of stock at a gentle simmer. Gradually add the remaining stock as it is absorbed by the rice, and stirring frequently. Test the rice after 18 minutes and, if it is not done, cook it for a little longer, still stirring so that it does not stick on the bottom of the pan.

5 Add the white wine, sage, Parmesan, chargrilled onion, asparagus, courgettes, mushrooms and pumpkin and the remaining butter to the pan. Mix well and cook for 3 minutes – the risotto should have a creamy texture – then serve, garnished with Parmesan shavings and chopped sage.

Serves 4
Preparation time: 15 minutes
Cooking time: 45 minutes

CHICORY WITH PARMESAN

4 chicory heads
100 g (3½ oz) Parmesan cheese, grated
sea salt and pepper
salad leaves, to serve

1 Heat the chargriller.

2 Slice the chicory heads in half lengthways, place them on the chargriller and cook for 2 minutes on each side. Repeat until all the chicory is cooked.

3 Place the chargrilled chicory in an ovenproof dish, season with salt and pepper and sprinkle with the grated Parmesan. Place the dish under a preheated conventional grill until the Parmesan is just bubbling. Serve immediately, accompanied by salad leaves.

Serves 4
Preparation time: 5 minutes
Cooking time: 10 minutes

AUBERGINE WRAPS

I large aubergine
2 red onions, thinly sliced
125 g (4 oz) Gruyère cheese, thinly sliced
2 beefsteak tomatoes, skinned and sliced
olive oil, for drizzling
sea salt and pepper
chopped chives, to garnish
radicchio salad, to serve

1 Heat the chargriller.

2 Cut the aubergine lengthways into thin slices, put them on the chargriller and cook for 3 minutes on each side. Remove and keep warm. Place the red onion slices on the chargriller and cook for 4 minutes on each side.

3 To assemble the wraps, take the 4 best slices of aubergine and put them on a plate. Towards one end of each piece of aubergine, place slices of Gruyère, red onion and tomato. Season with salt and pepper then fold the other end of the aubergine over the top. Garnish the wraps with the chopped chives and serve with a radicchio salad and the extra aubergine slices, drizzled with olive oil.

Serves 4
Preparation time: 8 minutes
Cooking time: 20 minutes

OPEN VEGETABLE TART WITH PARMESAN

This dish is both delicious and easy, and various vegetables can be used,
as you prefer. It is especially good either hot or cold on a warm summer's day with a green salad.

1 red onion
1 red pepper
1 leek
2 flat mushrooms
1 small fennel bulb
1 small aubergine or 4 baby aubergines
1 courgette
2 garlic cloves, peeled but left whole
1 bunch of basil
a drizzle of olive oil
75 g (3 oz) Parmesan, coarsely grated
sea salt and pepper

PASTRY:
175 g (6 oz) self-raising flour
50 g (2 oz) butter, softened
1 teaspoon dried mixed herbs
75 ml (3 fl oz) water
75 ml (3 fl oz) olive oil

1 Cook all the vegetables before making the pastry. Cut them into wedges, halves or slices and chargrill until lightly patched with black. Chargrill the garlic cloves whole and then cut them into slices.

2 To make the pastry, combine the flour and butter in a food processor, or by hand, until all the butter is mixed in. Add the herbs, water and oil, and process to form a dough ball. Turn out the dough on to a lightly floured surface and knead until smooth.

3 Lightly oil a baking sheet and gently press out the dough to form a circle about 25–30 cm (10–12 inches) in diameter.

4 Arrange the chargrilled vegetables over the dough, pressing them in gently. Strip the leaves from the basil, then add to the tart. Drizzle with olive oil, season well with salt and pepper and sprinkle with Parmesan. Bake in a preheated oven, 200°C (400°F), Gas Mark 6, for 12–15 minutes, until the dough is risen and golden.

Serves 4–6
Preparation time: 30 minutes
Cooking time: 40 minutes

CHARGRILLED CAKES WITH ICE CREAM AND MAPLE SYRUP

1 large egg
3 dessertspoons vegetable oil
75 g (3 oz) self-raising flour
15 g (½ oz) sugar
150 ml (¼ pint) milk
8 scoops of ice cream, such as vanilla
or chocolate
bottled maple syrup, to serve

1 To make the cake batter, put the egg, oil, flour, sugar and milk into a food processor or blender and process until it reaches a smooth creamy consistency.

2 Heat the chargriller to a moderate heat. Take one-third of the batter, divide it into 4 cakes on the chargriller, to make 4 cakes. After about 1 minute, the bottoms of the cakes will form a crust, the tops will start to set and air bubbles will rise. Using a fish slice, carefully turn them over and cook on the other side for 1 minute. Repeat twice more until all the batter is used – making 12 cakes in all.

3 Serve 3 cakes per person, with scoops of ice cream and maple sauce drizzled over the top.

Serves 4
Preparation time: 10 minutes
Cooking time: 10 minutes

SWEET BRUSCHETTA WITH PLUMS AND CINNAMON

75 g (3 oz) brown sugar
3 tablespoons water
75 g (3 oz) butter
8 plums, more if they are small
4 slices of bread
150 g (5 oz) Greek yogurt
ground cinnamon, for dusting

1 Place the sugar, water and butter in a small saucepan and simmer to make a smooth caramel sauce. Remove from the heat and set aside.

2 Heat the chargriller. Cut the plums in half, remove the stones if they are large or leave them whole if they are small. Put them on the chargriller and cook for 5 minutes, turning constantly.

3 Toast the bread on the chargriller or in a toaster.

4 Arrange the toast on 4 plates, add the chargrilled plums and Greek yogurt. Spoon over the caramel sauce and dust the plums with cinnamon.

Serves 4
Preparation time: 10 minutes
Cooking time: 10 minutes

CHARGRILLED PEARS WITH CHOCOLATE SAUCE

4 pears
50 g (2 oz) flaked almonds, toasted

CHOCOLATE SAUCE:
175 g (6 oz) good quality dark chocolate
3 tablespoons water
I tablespoon golden syrup
15 g (½ oz) butter

1 To make the chocolate sauce, first make a bain-marie. Half fill a small saucepan with water, then fit an ovenproof bowl into the saucepan so that the bottom of the bowl is just immersed in the water. Place the bain-marie on the heat and let the water simmer gently. Add the chocolate, water, golden syrup and butter, allow to melt and mix together until the chocolate sauce is glossy and smooth.

2 Heat the chargriller.

3 Peel the pears, if liked, cut them into quarters and core. Place on the chargriller and cook for 2–3 minutes on each side.

4 Serve the chargrilled pears with the chocolate sauce drizzled over, and sprinkled with flaked almonds. To make this a really wicked pudding, serve it with a spoonful of clotted cream or a scoop of ice cream.

Serves 4
Preparation time: 10 minutes
Cooking time: 10–15 minutes

CHARGRILLED FIGS WITH GREEK YOGURT AND HONEY

Warm figs with Greek yogurt and honey drizzled over them make a delicious and quick dessert.
Buy figs when they are in season, when they are juicy and full of flavour.

8 ripe figs
4 tablespoons Greek yogurt
2 tablespoons clear honey

1 Heat the chargriller.

2 Put the figs on the chargriller and cook for 8 minutes, turning occasionally, until they are charred on the outside. Remove and cut in half.

3 Arrange the figs on 4 plates and serve with a spoonful of Greek yogurt and some honey spooned over the top.

Serves 4
Preparation time: 5 minutes
Cooking time: 10 minutes

CHARGRILLED STRAWBERRIES ON ICE CREAM

This recipe works equally well with fresh cherries or plums.

500 g (1 lb) strawberries, washed but unhulled
500 ml (17 fl oz) luxury ice cream, such as vanilla, strawberry or chocolate, to serve

1 Heat the chargriller. Place the strawberries on the chargriller and cook for 3–4 minutes, turning frequently.
2 While the strawberries are cooking, scoop the ice cream into 4 individual dishes. Spoon the chargrilled strawberries on top and serve immediately.

Serves 4
Preparation time: 5 minutes
Cooking time: 3–4 minutes

PINEAPPLE WITH HAZELNUTS AND CREME FRAICHE

Pineapple works very well on the chargriller because of its high natural sugar content, which produces really dramatic grill lines.

1 pineapple, peeled, halved lengthways and sliced
125 g (4 oz) roasted hazelnuts, chopped
125 g (4 oz) crème fraîche

1 Heat the chargriller.
2 Place the pineapple slices on the chargriller and cook for 1–2 minutes on each side.
3 Mix the hazelnuts into the crème fraîche.
4 Serve the chargrilled pineapple with the nutty crème fraîche spooned over it.

Serves 4
Preparation time: 10 minutes
Cooking time: 5 minutes

INDEX